Joseph
STALIN

BROWNING

No .... — ....   Class ....

Author .. — ....

Title ...... — ....

BRISTOL CITY COUNCIL LIBRARY SERVICE
PLEASE RETURN BOOK BY LAST DATE STAMPED

30 OCT 07

29 JUL 04

29. JUL

AUG

7 NOV 2019

BRISTOL CITY COUNCIL
LIBRARY SERVICES
WITHDRAWN AND OFFERED FOR SALE
SOLD AS SEEN

BR100

KU-525-655

BRISTOL CITY LIBRARIES

AN2659161 8

	29-Oct-02
084	£7.50
	SA

BE

BE
8/06

Bristol Library Service
Renewals 0117 903 7240

Heinemann
LIBRARY

AN 2659161 8

H www.heinemann.co.uk/library
Visit our website to find out more information about Heinemann Library books.

To order:
☎ Phone 44 (0) 1865 888066
▤ Send a fax to 44 (0) 1865 314091
▢ Visit the Heinemann Bookshop at www.heinemann.co.uk/library to browse our catalogue and order online.

First published in Great Britain by Heinemann Library,
Halley Court, Jordan Hill, Oxford OX2 8EJ,
a division of Reed Educational and Professional Publishing Ltd.
Heinemann is a registered trademark of Reed Educational and Professional Publishing Ltd.

OXFORD MELBOURNE AUCKLAND
JOHANNESBURG BLANTYRE GABORONE
IBADAN PORTSMOUTH (NH) USA CHICAGO

© Reed Educational and Professional Publishing Ltd 2002
The moral right of the proprietor has been asserted.

All rights reserved. No part of this publication may be reproduced, stored in a retrieval system, or transmitted in any form or by any means, electronic, mechanical, photocopying, recording, or otherwise, without either the prior written permission of the publishers or a licence permitting restricted copying in the United Kingdom issued by the Copyright Licensing Agency Ltd, 90 Tottenham Court Road, London W1P 0LP.

Designed by AMR
Illustrated by Art Construction
Originated by Dot Gradations
Printed in China

ISBN 0 431 13855 9 (hardback)   ISBN 0 431 13862 1 (paperback)
05 04 03 02 01   06 05 04 03 02
10 9 8 7 6 5 4 3 2 1   10 9 8 7 6 5 4 3 2 1

British Library Cataloguing in Publication Data
Downing, David
   Joseph Stalin. – (Leading lives)
   1.Stalin, I. (Iosif), 1879–1953 – Juvenile literature
   2.Heads of state – Soviet Union – Biography – Juvenile
   literature 3.Soviet Union – Politics and government –
   1936–1953 – Juvenile literature 4.Soviet Union – History –
   1925–1953 – Juvenile literature
   I.Title
   947'.0842'092

Acknowledgements
The publishers would like to thank the following for permission to reproduce photographs:
AKG: pp. 5, 47, 48; Corbis: pp. 6, 22, 23, 54; David King: pp. 7, 36; Hulton Getty: pp. 8, 11, 17, 19, 45; Novosti: pp. 4, 12, 15, 20, 25, 30, 31, 33, 43, 50; PA Photos: p. 55; Popperfoto: pp. 28, 34, 35, 39, 51.

Cover photograph reproduced with permission of Hulton Getty.

Our thanks to Christopher Gibb for his comments in the preparation of this book.

Every effort has been made to contact copyright holders of any material reproduced in this book. Any omissions will be rectified in subsequent printings if notice is given to the publishers.

Any words appearing in the text in bold, **like this**, are explained in the Glossary.

Contents

The man of steel

We are in Red Square on a beautiful autumn day in Moscow, in October 1935. It is the eighteenth anniversary of the Russian Revolution, and thousands upon thousands of marchers are parading through the square. Some carry portraits of Vladimir Ilyich Lenin, the leader of that revolution, but many more are holding up huge pictures of another man, one with dark sleeked-back hair, a large moustache and narrowed, suspicious eyes.

This man is standing on a platform below the high walls and soaring towers of Moscow's **Kremlin** fortress. Since 1929 he has ruled the new Russia, the 'Soviet Union', virtually alone. His name is Stalin, which in Russian means 'man of steel'.

When he dies in 1953 he will be remembered as the maker of modern Russia, and as one of the most murderous **dictators**

in history. But at this moment, in 1935, the radio and the newspapers never stop singing his praises. He is the 'shining sun of humanity', 'the father of us all'. Once 'Lenin's closest collaborator', he has become 'the greatest man of all times, all epochs, all peoples'.

▲ *A military parade in Moscow's Red Square forms part of the 1935 May Day celebrations.*

What crosses Stalin's mind when he reads such things? Does he think about his hopes for the distant future – that perfect world he claims he will one day bring about for his people? Or is he thinking about the millions who follow his orders, working long days and nights to make that future possible? Perhaps, on this day of all days, he is remembering the other men and women who shared in the making of the revolution they are celebrating, most of whom are now rotting in his jails. Or is he thinking back still further, to his own years as an outlaw, to all the nights in hiding and days on the run?

▲ Joseph Stalin, born Joseph Djugashvili, in 1936.

Does he even spare a thought for his two dead wives, his three children, or his mother far away in Soviet Georgia, who still wishes he had become a priest? Perhaps as he gazes stonily down at the marching lines of neatly uniformed schoolchildren, his mind wanders back to the long-ago days of his own childhood….

A serious case of hero worship

'All thanks to thee, O Great Educator, Stalin. I love a young woman with a renewed love and shall perpetuate myself in my children, all thanks to thee, O Great Educator, Stalin. I shall be eternally happy and joyous, all thanks to thee, O Great Educator, Stalin. Everything belongs to thee, chief of our great country. And when the woman I love presents me with a child the first word it shall utter will be "Stalin".'

(From a **delegate's** speech to the Soviet parliament, 1935)

Childhood and youth

▲ *The small two-room house in the Georgian town of Gori in which Stalin grew up.*

On 6 December 1878 a third son was born to Vissarion and Ektarina Djugashvili in Gori, a small town in the Russian province of Georgia. Their first two boys had died as babies but this one, called Soso (Georgian for Joseph), survived.

Vissarion earned his living making shoes at home for a business in the Georgian capital, Tiflis, but he also drank too much, and times were never easy in the small two-room house which the family shared. It was Ektarina who made sure that the family rarely went hungry. She took in washing and did housework for richer families in the town. In the early years of their marriage Vissarion frequently beat both Ektarina and Soso, but eventually Ektarina started fighting back, and Vissarion left to live in Tiflis.

Gori

The young Soso grew up in the small town, with its hot summers, rushing river and panoramic views of snow-covered mountains. He went with his mother to the weekly market; he watched the steam trains puff their way down the valley. At the age of 5 or 6 he caught **smallpox**, and although he survived he was left with a permanently pock-marked face.

He started at the town's church school, where he sang in the choir, enjoyed boxing, and was considered the star pupil. He became the leader of a small gang of children, and 60 years later, at the height of World War II, he still felt fond enough of these childhood friends to send them all money. These were probably the happiest years of his life.

His father disappeared completely when Soso was about 11 and his mother was left to make the decisions about his future. She wanted him to become a priest, partly because she was religious herself, partly because it was one of the few good jobs that poor Georgian people could hope to get. She fixed him up with a place at the most important religious school in Georgia – the Tiflis theological seminary – and his Gori headmaster helped arrange a scholarship which would pay for his clothes, food and lodging. In 1893, at the age of 15, Soso took the train to the capital.

▶ *Soso Djugashvili (back row, fourth from the left) with his classmates.*

The seminary

The seminary was very different from the church school. He found religious studies boring, and the discipline was much stricter than he was used to. The seminary had recently been closed for a while because of student troubles, and the teachers still did not trust their students, who were rarely allowed out into the town and were continually spied on.

Soso's rebellious instincts soon showed through. At first he was content to write fiery romantic poetry and read about the heroic adventures of Koba, a Georgian Robin Hood from years gone by, but after a year or so he became interested in more up-to-date rebels – the **Socialists**. He and other students formed a secret Socialist discussion group in the seminary, and then they joined one of the more **revolutionary** groups in the city outside. They visited groups of workers and shared their vision of a Socialist world, one that was fairer for everyone.

Soso was better at winning followers than making friends. His fellow students quickly learnt that he did not like losing arguments.

▲ Soso Djugashvili as a student of the Tiflis seminary in 1894.

They also understood that he bore grudges against those who defeated him in discussions. He soon stopped caring about his college work, preferring to read books that were forbidden. He argued with his teachers, and was often rude. In the spring of 1899 he failed to turn up for some examinations, and the teachers used this as an excuse to expel him.

First and last job

Soso was 20 years old now, and he did not go back to Gori. That summer and autumn he did a little private teaching, and towards the end of the year he got his first and only non-political job, as a worker at the Tiflis observatory. On the night when the 19th century gave way to the 20th he was alone at the telescope, taking notes on the behaviour of the heavens.

Politics were the most important thing in his life. When, fifteen months later, a big demonstration was planned in the city, Soso was one of the main organizers. The police knew it, but when they arrived at the observatory to arrest him, he was gone. For the next sixteen years his only permanent homes would be in prison or **exile**.

'RUSSIA'

In 1900 the Russian Empire included **European Russia**, most of Poland, the vast Asian region known as Siberia, and present-day Finland, Lithuania, Latvia, Estonia, Moldova, Belarus, Ukraine, Georgia, Azerbaijan, Armenia, Turkmenistan, Kazakhstan, Uzbekistan, Kirghizstan and Tadjikistan. Finland and Poland became independent states in 1917 and 1918. The rest remained part of the Union of Soviet Socialist Republics (or Soviet Union) until its break-up in the early 1990s.

TO LOCATE THE PLACES MENTIONED, SEE THE MAP OF THE RUSSIAN EMPIRE ON PAGE 13.

3 The revolutionary

The first stop on Joseph Djugashvili's journey as a **revolutionary** was Batum, a small seaport on the Georgian Black Sea coast (see map on page 13). Once there he slept on the floors and sofas of sympathizers, helped print revolutionary newspapers in concealed cellars, and braved police checks with his forged documents. He gave talks to groups of workers about **Socialism**, always wondering if the police were about to come crashing through the door.

Who was Djugashvili – the future Stalin – working for? In 1898 the Russian Social Democratic Workers Party had been formed, and the small group of **Marxist Socialists**, which he had joined in Tiflis, soon became part of this bigger party. All this activity was illegal – such political parties were not allowed in the empire of the **czar**. Revolutionaries like Djugashvili thought of themselves as soldiers in a secret army, and knew that they were likely to spend much of their lives either behind bars or **exiled** to some distant Siberian outpost.

For details on key people of Stalin's time, see pages 58–9.

In early 1902 Djugashvili was one of the main organizers of a violent demonstration in which at least fifteen workers were killed, and the police finally caught up with him. He was locked up in Batum prison and then sent into exile. During this time, the Russian Social Democratic Workers Party split into two halves, the **Bolsheviks** and the **Mensheviks**. The Bolsheviks, under their leader Lenin, were more willing than the Mensheviks to wage a ruthless **underground war** against the authorities. When Djugashvili heard about the split he knew whose side he was on. He had no doubts that the Bolsheviks' ruthless action was what was needed.

Marxist Socialism

Karl Marx was a 19th-century German philosopher who believed he had worked out how society changes. He thought that throughout history each ruling class – each group of people who dominated a society through either force or wealth or a combination of the two – inevitably created their own opposition. In his time the **bourgeoisie** – the owners of industry and communications and banks – were the ruling class in the most advanced countries, but to make their world work they needed a growing army of ordinary workers.

Marx believed that these workers would eventually get so numerous and so fed up with making wealth for other people that they would kick out the bourgeoisie and rule in their place. Since the workers would then be a big majority of the population, their rule would be fairer for most people. It would be called Socialism.

Marx had many facts to back up his theory, and many people came to believe that he was right in his predictions. They were called Marxists or Marxist Socialists.

▲ *Photographs of Joseph Djugashvili – the future Stalin – taken in around 1912–13 for the records of the* **czarist** *secret police.*

First exile, first marriage

Though thin and no more than 1 metre and 57 centimetres tall, Djugashvili proved a brave prisoner, enduring the beatings he was given in a contemptuous silence. After eighteen months he was exiled to the province of Irkutsk in Siberia, some 4800 kilometres (3000 miles) away. A first attempt at escape brought him nothing more than a frostbitten nose and ears, but the second attempt was successful, and by January 1904 he was back in Tiflis.

It was probably in this year that he met and married Ektarina Svanidze. She was the sister of another revolutionary, but she was religious and uninterested in politics. She insisted that they marry in church, and he agreed, even though the Bolsheviks were violently opposed to religion. For the next few years he seems to have led even more of a double life than usual. On the one hand, he tried, in almost impossible circumstances, to live a normal family life with a woman he obviously loved; on the other, he continued with his secret and always dangerous work as a revolutionary.

Lenin's fund-raiser

1905 was a year of great political upheavals in the Russian Empire, but Djugashvili's part of the country was quieter than most. In December he finally met Lenin, who seems to have realized that Djugashvili was both competent and prepared to do almost anything for the party. He was given the job of raising money by carrying out robberies in his home territory of the Caucasus.

▲ Stalin's first wife, Ektarina Svanidze, who did not share his interest in revolutionary politics.

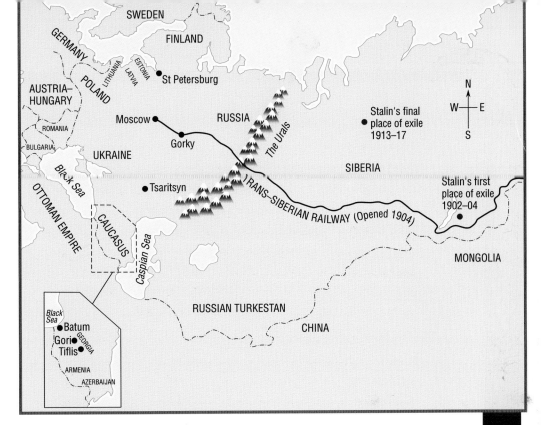

▲ *The Russian Empire c. 1900.*

The most famous of these robberies took place in Tiflis's Erevan Square on 26 June 1907. A gold shipment and its **Cossack** guard were suddenly attacked by about 50 revolutionaries armed with bombs and guns. When the smoke cleared, many soldiers and innocent passers-by could be seen lying dead or wounded on the ground, but Djugashvili's men and the gold were gone.

This success, and the others which followed it, must have pleased Djugashvili, but that same year his own life was marked by tragedy. Soon after giving birth to their son Yakov, Ektarina fell ill. It was dangerous to visit her too often, and he had no money to pay for treatment. Eventually he managed to have her moved back to her own family, but it was too late. At her funeral Djugashvili told an old friend that she had 'softened his stony heart', and that all his warm feelings for humanity had died with her.

Djugashvili left his son Yakov to be brought up by Ektarina's sister, and he threw himself back into his work. He was soon arrested. A year later he escaped, only to be recaptured after six months. Again he escaped, again he was arrested. Each time, he was sent further into the Siberian wilderness, with its long freezing winters and short hot summers.

Nationalities

In the winter of 1912–13, during one of his short spells at liberty, Djugashvili met Lenin in the Austrian capital, Vienna. Lenin knew that although Djugashvili was not a great speaker or thinker, he was from a poor family, and the party needed people who understood the struggle to make ends meet. Lenin particularly liked Djugashvili's no-nonsense attitude, the way he got things done. He was also useful to

Djugashvili in Vienna

'The door opened without a knock, and a strange figure appeared on the threshold: a very thin man, rather short, his face swarthy with a greyish tinge and clearly visible pockmarks. He looked anything but friendly. This stranger made a grunting sound, which might have been taken for a greeting, silently poured himself a glass of tea, and just as silently left the room.'

(Leon Trotsky (see page 59) on his first sighting of his future rival, 1913)

Lenin as a Georgian. Only two-thirds of those who lived in the Russian Empire were Russians, and if the Bolsheviks ever seized power they would have to deal with the other third, peoples like the Ukrainians and Armenians, Uzbeks and Georgians. Lenin asked Djugashvili to help him decide the party's policy towards these people. In early 1913, Djugashvili wrote his first important essay, 'Marxism and the National

Question'. He was now one of the party's experts and a member of its **Central Committee**. He gave himself a new name, 'Stalin'.

Last exile

Soon after his return to Russia, Stalin was arrested and exiled once more. World War I began in 1914, but Stalin spent most of his time fishing and hunting for the food he needed to keep himself alive. His life was often boring, usually miserable, and sometimes terrifying. One day he got lost in a blizzard and almost froze to death.

Then, early in 1917, incredible news reached Siberia – a revolution was spreading like wildfire across **European Russia**. The exiles scrambled aboard westbound trains, eager to play their part. Many of them, like Stalin, had spent their whole adult lives working and waiting for this moment.

▲ *The house in Siberia where Stalin lived during his final period in exile.*

Power

FOR DETAILS ON KEY PEOPLE OF STALIN'S TIME, SEE PAGES 58–9.

The revolution in February 1917 that overthrew the **czar** should, according to the predictions of Karl Marx, have been a '**bourgeois**' revolution, putting the business and middle classes in power. The **Socialist** revolution could only come much later, once the middle classes had developed industry and increased the number of ordinary workers. So, for the moment, it was the duty of **Marxist Socialists** to support the 'bourgeois' revolution, and this was what Stalin and other **Bolsheviks** did once they reached the city of Petrograd (**St Petersburg**) and started publishing the party newspaper, *Pravda* (*Truth*).

Lenin, though, had other ideas. When he reached Russia in March he announced a complete change of policy. The Bolsheviks should aim for a Socialist revolution immediately, he announced. He agreed that Russia was not ready for one, but argued that richer countries like Germany were, and that a Bolshevik takeover in Russia would encourage revolution both there and everywhere else. Stalin was surprised by this change of policy, but he was tempted by the possibility of power, just as Lenin and his great ally Trotsky were.

A confusion of names

The Bolsheviks originally called themselves Marxist Socialists. According to Marx, a **Communist** society was the perfect society that would follow a Socialist one. The Bolsheviks started using the name Communists to distinguish themselves from other Socialists who were not as ready to use violence and other undemocratic methods as they were. They officially changed their name to the Russian Communist Party in 1918.

If that is confusing, it may be some consolation to know that most of those involved found it confusing too. Some of these words have been virtually interchangeable ever since!

One Bolshevik attempt to seize power in June was defeated, but another in October proved successful. Stalin's main task in this, the second Russian revolution of 1917, was to make sure that Lenin escaped if everything went wrong. He was now a member of the party's four-man leadership committee, and someone whom Lenin particularly relied on.

Civil war and new love

The Bolsheviks became the government, but many people in Russia refused to recognize their authority, and by early 1918 a **civil war** was raging between the **Red Army** (Bolsheviks) and the **White Army** (their opponents). All the normal arrangements for transporting food broke down and Stalin was sent south in an armoured train to the city of Tsaritsyn. His job was to get wheat delivered to the hungry cities of Moscow and Petrograd. He had 400 **Red Guards** with him, and once in Tsaritsyn he waged a **reign of terror** against anyone involved with the **black market** in food. Thousands were shot, and many hidden grain stores were found. When a White Army attacked the city, Stalin successfully organized its defence. (Seven years later it would be re-named Stalingrad in his honour.)

TO LOCATE THE PLACES MENTIONED, SEE THE MAP OF THE RUSSIAN EMPIRE ON PAGE 13.

▶ *Stalin at the Eighth Congress of the Russian Communist Party, March 1919. By this time he held several important posts in both party and government.*

Stalin's secretary in Tsaritsyn was Nadezhda Alliluyeva, the daughter of another Bolshevik, whom Stalin had known since his Tiflis days. She was impressed by the hard and apparently romantic life he had led, and he was struck by her youth and innocence. Although there were twenty years between their ages, she became his wife.

He was sent north to Petrograd, and then south once more to the Ukraine. He seemed to have a knack of coping with military and political crises, although some of his fellow Bolsheviks – Trotsky in particular – thought he was unimaginative and relied too much on simple brutality. As far as Lenin was concerned, what worked was all that mattered. If the civil war was lost then they would all be slaughtered.

Positions of power

Stalin had other jobs beside the military ones – jobs which became much more important once the civil war had been won. He was the **Commissar for Nationalities** in the government, with the responsibility of persuading the non-Russian peoples to stay within the new Soviet Union. He used both promises and threats: the non-Russians were offered partly self-governing, **autonomous** republics inside the Union, but any who tried to break away and set up their own countries quickly received a visit from the Red Army.

Stalin was a member of the most powerful committees in the party. He was on the ruling seven-man **Politburo** and he was a member of another committee which supervised the **political police**. Most important of all, he was a leading figure in the party Secretariat, which controlled who got which party jobs. When the post of general secretary was created early in

1922, Lenin chose Stalin to fill it, partly because no one else wanted such an apparently boring job, partly because Lenin knew that Stalin would do it with his usual efficiency. The Georgian always got things done.

Stalin was responsible for appointing local party secretaries throughout the country, and they chose the people who were sent to Moscow to serve on all the important committees. In the future, when there were disputes over policy, or disagreements about who should lead the party, Stalin would be able to count on a great deal of support.

▼ *General Secretary Stalin walking down a Moscow street with Commissar for the Economy (and fellow Georgian) Sergo Ordzhonikidze in 1924.*

The succession struggle

▲ *Stalin visits the convalescing Lenin in the village of Gorky during 1922.*

Lenin became seriously ill late in 1921, and by the middle of the following year he was forced to take a long holiday from work and responsibility. He went to stay in Gorky, a village about 30 kilometres (20 miles) south of the new capital Moscow. Stalin was his most frequent visitor.

Things were going well for the Georgian. The war was over, and he had one of the most important jobs in the country. He and Nadezhda had moved into a house in Moscow. It was the first proper home of his adult life. They had a new son, Vasili, and in 1921 Yakov, the son from his first marriage whom he had hardly seen for fifteen years, came to live with them.

Lenin's illness, though, was a dark cloud on his horizon. Stalin had always been Lenin's man, and he knew he would have to fight for his political life against the other **Bolshevik** leaders when Lenin died. He may also have discovered that Lenin now regretted giving him so much power, an issue Lenin raised in his 'Testament' (a Letter to the Party Congress and postscript).

Last words

'Having become general secretary, Comrade Stalin has concentrated unlimited power in his hands, and I am not sure that he will always use that power with sufficient care. ...
*'Stalin is too rude and this failing, which is entirely acceptable in relations among us **Communists**, is not acceptable in a general secretary. I therefore suggest that the comrades find a means of moving Stalin from this post and giving the job to someone else who is superior to Comrade Stalin in every way, that is, more patient, more loyal, more respectful and more considerate to his comrades....'*

(Excerpts from Lenin's 'Testament', written in December 1922 and January 1923)

A narrow escape

Lenin died in January 1924, and his Testament was finally read to the **Central Committee** at the party's Thirteenth Congress in May. Stalin was not the only one whom Lenin criticized, but he was the only one whom the old leader suggested should be sacked. Most of those present were embarrassed for Stalin. 'He looked small and miserable,' one eyewitness wrote later; 'in spite of his self-control and show of calm it was clearly evident that his fate was at stake.'

This was one of the key moments of the 20th century. Had the other leaders insisted on upholding Lenin's wishes, the future of the Soviet Union and the rest of the world would probably have been very different. But for reasons of their own they allowed him to keep his job, little realizing that one day he would use it to kill them all.

Differences

Why did they do this? One reason was that the other Bolshevik leaders were split along lines of both personality and policy. They did not like each other very much, and they did not agree with each other when it came to deciding what they should do next with their revolution. Trotsky was the most famous and the most able of them, but he was also the most conceited (as Lenin had pointed out in his Testament). The others did not like the way he talked down to them, and they were afraid he would try to use his influence with the **Red Army** to seize power on his own. Even those who agreed with Trotsky's ideas for the revolution, like the popular Zinoviev, were scared of supporting him too wholeheartedly. These people allowed Stalin to survive – at least in part – because they felt they needed him and his supporters as a counter-balance to Trotsky.

For details on key people of Stalin's time, see pages 58–9.

▲ *Leon Trotsky, Stalin's principal adversary in the period surrounding Lenin's death.*

There were also those, like Bukharin, who opposed Trotsky because they disagreed with his ideas. The Bolsheviks had originally justified their revolution by saying that it would encourage revolutions elsewhere, but these had not happened. Trotsky said that they should carry on trying to make trouble in the rest of the world (he called this a policy of 'permanent revolution'), but Bukharin and his allies thought the Bolsheviks had to get used to the idea that they had to concentrate on their own revolution. Their job was to do whatever they could in Russia, to build '**Socialism** in one country'.

Stalin supported Bukharin's policy, partly because this had also been Lenin's position, and partly because it seemed to make more practical sense than Trotsky's. In return Bukharin and his allies were happy to offer Stalin support when he most needed it.

The way forward
Once Stalin had survived Lenin's Testament he went from strength to strength. With Bukharin and his allies he always had a majority on the important committees, and Trotsky and Zinoviev were continually outvoted. 'Socialism in one country' became the party's official goal.

▲ *Stalin accompanied by fellow party leaders Alexei Rykov, Lev Kamenev and Grigori Zinoviev in June 1925.*

Now that the destination of establishing Socialism in Russia had been decided, the leaders began arguing about how best to reach it. It needed industry and workers, but the only people who could pay for the necessary expansion of Russian industry – supply the food for the cities and the labour for the factories – were the people who now lived in the countryside, the **peasants**, who still made up more than 90 per cent of the population. Lenin had wanted to encourage the peasants to produce more food and make more money. He hoped that they would spend this money on **industrial goods** and thereby stimulate the expansion of industry. It would be a slow process but he was convinced that eventually it would work.

Fast or slow?

Stalin and Bukharin carried on supporting this policy after Lenin's death, but Trotsky and Zinoviev thought that things should be speeded up. They were not convinced that the peasants would do what was expected of them, and they were also afraid that the party, by encouraging what Trotsky called 'the devil of the market', would allow the **bourgeoisie** to recover some of its power. They argued that the peasants should be paid less for their food than the **market rate**. The towns would make a profit, which they could use to build industries, and the peasants would have no choice but to come and work in them if they wanted a decent living.

This argument could be heard at hundreds of party meetings in the mid-1920s, but the 'slow' approach favoured by Stalin and Bukharin remained the official policy, at least for the moment. Stalin was always careful to make sure he had majority support when a vote was called for, and he was quite prepared to postpone meetings when it looked like he might lose.

He was good at arguing his case as well. He was not dramatic or clever like Trotsky, but thorough, logical and straightforward. He was good at picking out quotations from Lenin's writings to support his own views.

Stalin's home life during this period also seemed secure, and in 1926 Nadezhda gave birth to a daughter, Svetlana.

One left standing

As the years went by Stalin got more and more of his own supporters onto the Central Committee and the smaller **Politburo**. In early 1927 both Trotsky and Zinoviev were forced out of the leadership, and there seemed no one left to oppose the 'slow' approach, no one left to threaten Stalin and Bukharin's position.

This was not enough for Stalin. With what now seems almost incredible nerve, he suddenly changed his mind and came out in favour of the very policies for which he had condemned Trotsky and Zinoviev. Now it was Bukharin and his supporters who found themselves outvoted on committees packed with Stalin's supporters. Over the next two years they were forced out of their positions, leaving only Stalin at the summit of power.

▶ *Nikolai Bukharin, Stalin's chief ally during the years 1924–29.*

Why did Stalin adopt those policies which he had so recently opposed? He certainly wanted to get rid of Bukharin, who was the only other important leader left from Lenin's day, but there were other good reasons for the change of course. The outside threats to the Soviet Union seemed to be growing, and in the modern world a country needed industrial strength to defend itself. The slow way was too slow, and in any case the peasants were refusing to co-operate with the existing system, hoarding their grain and refusing to sell it to the cities. Stalin decided that if he was going to industrialize Russia he needed to take complete control – of the countryside, of the cities, of everything and everyone.

Key dates: Stalin's rise to power

1917	The Bolshevik Revolution
1918–21	Civil war
1922	Stalin becomes general secretary
1924	Lenin dies
1925–27	Stalin defeats Trotsky and Zinoviev
1927–29	Stalin defeats Bukharin

6 Modernization

The enormous upheaval which took place in Russia between 1927 and 1932 changed the country out of all recognition. It was not called a revolution, but it was one in all the ways that mattered, and Stalin was its leader.

In these years Stalin undertook the **modernization** of Russia, but it was not this alone – the growth of industries and communications and the mechanization of agriculture – which added up to a revolution. England, Germany, the USA and others had all been through such developments in the past. What turned Stalin's modernization programme into a revolution was the way it was done. Never before had a country modernized itself at such incredible speed or with such appalling disregard for the human consequences.

Farming

The first step was to control the **peasants**, and at the end of 1927 the **collectivization of agriculture** was announced. There would be no more private farms. Peasants would become workers on one of the new, huge collective farms, and would be paid a wage like any worker in the town. All animals and tools would belong to the collective. Machine tractor stations would be set up to provide tractors for each group of 40 farms. The harvest, in whole or part, would belong to the state. The local party officials would make all the decisions about what to grow and who did which jobs.

The richer farmers (called '**kulaks**') had the most to lose, and Stalin knew that they would fight his plans. In 1929 he announced that he was going to 'liquidate the kulaks as a social class', and over the next few years he kept his word.

The liquidation of the kulaks

'Trainloads of deported peasants left for the icy north, the forests, the steppes, the desert. These were whole populations, denuded of everything; the old folk starved in mid-journey, new-born babies were buried on the banks of the roadside, and each wilderness had its crop of little crosses of boughs or white wood.'

(A description from *Memoirs of a Revolutionary*, written by the **revolutionary** Victor Serge)

▲ A group of farm workers at a collective farm near Kharkov in the Ukraine.

Most of the kulaks were killed or sent to labour camps; even the luckiest ones were sent to poor farming areas. At least half a million peasants died in this first phase of collectivization, but many more than that died in the famines that followed. Rather than give up their animals to the collective farms, millions of peasants just killed and ate them. Rather than give up their crops, they burnt them. And then they starved.

Stalin now had the complete control over agriculture that he thought he needed to pay for industrialization. But he had made a lasting enemy of the countryside and its people, and Soviet agriculture would never really recover from these few terrible years.

Industry

The growth of industry was also completely controlled by the party. There was no room for private enterprise or market forces, no place for individual profits or the uncertainty of uncontrolled contacts with the world economy. The Russian economy was sealed off from the rest of the world, and almost everything that happened in it – buying, selling, producing, transporting – was planned down to the last detail.

If a new steelworks was planned, then one organization was ordered to supply the bricks and machinery, another to build the necessary roads and railways, another to ensure that enough workers were found to run the works once it was built. The central planners decided the level of wages, the sources of raw materials, the destination of the final product. This and every other industry was included in one great national plan.

There had been some rough planning in Russia since 1921, some rough notion of what the country needed and how the party should go about providing it, but this sort of detailed planning, covering the whole economy over a period of years, was completely new. It had never been tried before in any country.

The first **five-year plan**, which was introduced in 1928, was incredibly ambitious. Stalin tackled the basics first: he ordered a three-fold increase in the Soviet production of coal, iron, steel, oil and machinery in those five years. Once the country had achieved this, other industries, like the weapons industry, could be expanded in their turn. Stalin had not forgotten that the rest of the world was hostile to the lone **Communist** state. 'We are 50 to 100 years behind the advanced countries,' he said in 1931. 'We must make up this gap in ten years. Either we do this or they crush us.'

◀ Workers using picks and shovels to modernize the village of Magnitogorsk. In 1929 it had a population of just over 1000. Four years later it had steel mills and blast furnaces, shops and hospitals and schools, and a population of over 100,000.

A different world

Many Soviet people wanted to see their country modernized, and there was no shortage of enthusiasm or idealism among the hundreds of thousands who set off to build new dams on the huge rivers or construct cities like Magnitogorsk from scratch in the rugged Siberian wilderness. The work was hard, the wages poor, but the sense of achievement in transforming a country undoubtedly infected many of those involved.

Those who lacked enthusiasm still had to work. On many projects two absences from work meant time in jail; more than that meant

▼ *Stalin's second wife, Nadezhda Alliluyeva, sitting in the garden of Stalin's **dacha** around 1930.*

a spell in a **labour camp**. With everything planned to the last detail, economic freedom became a thing of the past. You worked where and how you were told to. Internal passports and labour books detailing an individual's work history were introduced to stop people moving around from place to place or job to job. Stalin's control over the life of the whole country became virtually complete.

However, there was one person Stalin could not control. Shocked by the sufferings in the countryside, his wife Nadezhda had become deeply depressed, and one evening in 1932, after a row with Stalin in front of guests, she stormed off to her room and shot herself. Stalin showed no grief for her death. Perhaps he had learned by this time to hide his feelings. Perhaps he no longer had any to hide.

Many people had their lives turned inside out by the **collectivization of agriculture** and the forced industrialization programme that began at the end of the 1920s. Some lost their land and their independence, and nearly everyone lost the freedom to do what they wanted and go where they wanted. Those who protested were arrested, and more often than not they ended up in prison or a **labour camp**. In 1930 a special department of the secret police was set up to run the growing number of camps. This department was called the Gulag.

Conditions in the labour camps were terrible. Most of them were situated in Siberia or the far north of **European Russia**, where the winters were long, dark and incredibly cold. The prisoners were forced to work long hours for pitifully small rations, and many died of hunger, **hypothermia** or simple exhaustion. In the early 1930s most of those sent to the camps were ordinary criminals, **peasants** who had opposed the collectivization, or workers who had failed to do the work required of them. But from 1934 onwards these groups were quickly outnumbered by the victims of the **purges**.

Kirov

Stalin had now been the country's undisputed leader for several years, and he must have felt more alone than ever. His wife was dead and he had fallen out with his older son Yakov, whom he considered weak. He hardly saw Vasili and Svetlana, his two children by Nadezhda. In the 1920s he had often spent evenings with his comrades and their wives, but after Nadezhda's death the wives were no longer invited. He now spent his time alone or with people who dared not contradict him. Everyone said they were loyal to him, but what were they saying behind his back? He worried that he had no real way of finding out what was going on.

▲ *Stalin with his two children by his second wife, Nadezhda: Vasili (born 1921) and Svetlana (born 1926). By the mid-1930s, Stalin hardly spent any time with his children.*

Then, at the Seventeenth Congress of the Russian Communist Party in early 1934, a surprising number of party members voted against his policies. Many were worried that the industrialization and collectivization programmes were going too fast, and that the cost in human lives was too high. There was even talk of replacing Stalin with Sergei Kirov, the popular leader of the party's Leningrad (**St Petersburg**) branch.

Stalin felt threatened, both personally and politically. Since he was certain that his policies were the right ones, he could convince himself that any attack on him was also an attack on the country's future. It seems likely that he was actually fond of Kirov, but he was not going to let human feelings get in the way of protecting his own and the Soviet Union's interests.

Stalin with
Leningrad party
boss Sergei Kirov.
Stalin used Kirov's
assassination as
his excuse for
launching the
Great Terror.

On 1 December 1934 Kirov was shot dead in Leningrad. No
indisputable evidence has ever been found to connect Stalin
with the murder, but there is no real doubt that he was
behind it. In one stroke he had got rid of his biggest rival and
created the excuse for going after all those others who had
dared to oppose him at the Seventeeth Congress.

Years of fear

FOR DETAILS
ON KEY
PEOPLE OF
STALIN'S TIME,
SEE PAGES
58–9.

Over the next five years, in what came to be called the Great
Purge or Great Terror, millions of party members and officials
were either sent to the camps or executed. Old colleagues of
Stalin like Zinoviev and Bukharin, who had already been
removed from positions of power, were now given public 'show
trials' in which they confessed to all sorts of ridiculous crimes
which they had not committed. There were several explanations
for these confessions. Some confessed to save their families,
some because they hoped to save themselves, some because

they still wanted to believe that the party they had supported all their lives could not be wrong. They were all found 'guilty' and executed.

These show trials were just the tip of the iceberg. Fear gripped the whole country, and many people took the opportunity to settle old scores. Neighbours reported neighbours, children reported their own parents. It was no longer safe to say what you thought to anyone. Thousands of people heard the dreaded knock on their door in the middle of the night that meant the secret police had come to take them away. Even Trotsky, now far away in Mexico, was tracked down and killed. If Stalin was to sleep safely in his bed, then no one else could.

▲ Workers at a Moscow factory listen as an official reads a party bulletin denouncing Bukharin and his co-defendants at the 1938 show trial.

▲ *A Russian magazine cover showing Stalin as a star in the sky.*

A man alone

With the **reign of terror** came the **personality cult**. Stalin was everything and everywhere. His face appeared on billboards, covered whole buildings. It was even projected onto the clouds above. His bust or portrait adorned offices, factories, ordinary living rooms. Factories, streets, hospitals, rivers and towns were named after him. Plays, films, poems and novels celebrated his 'universal genius'. He was there to look after his children, in whatever way they deserved. God-like, he offered a clear choice: the heaven of working for a **Communist** future or the hell of the labour camps.

Who was the man inside this self-proclaimed god? The one thing we know is that he was essentially alone, and remained that way until the end. He travelled in his bullet-proof limousine along roads that had been cleared of people, arrived by train at empty, echoing station platforms. He had more than ten homes, each with its staff of servants forever waiting for an unannounced arrival.

Stalin's trip to the cinema

'One day Stalin decides to go to the cinema in disguise and hear what people are really saying about him. When the newsreel comes on the audience stand up and applaud each time he appears on the screen. Stalin is pleased. Modestly, he himself stays seated. After a few moments the man next to him leans over and whispers: "Most people feel the same way you do, Comrade, but you'll be safer if you stand up."'

(A Russian joke from the 1930s)

Stalin spent most of his days working and brooding at either the **Kremlin** or one of his country houses, or **dachas**. Most of his evenings featured long social dinners with the men he trusted most – those party leaders like Molotov, Voroshilov, Kaganovich and Beria, who owed their positions completely to him. He liked watching movies, and was particularly fond of Charlie Chaplin, but he had few other hobbies or interests. He could have had anything he wanted in the way of luxuries, but such things did not interest him. He was only really interested in power over others, and the contentment he derived from that was always tinged with the fear that it might be taken away.

Inhuman

'He is unhappy at not being able to convince everyone, himself included, that he is greater than everyone else, and this unhappiness of his may be his most human trait, perhaps the only human trait in him. But what is not human... is that because of this unhappiness he cannot avoid taking revenge on people... if someone speaks better than he does, that man is for it! Stalin will not let him live, because that man is a constant reminder that he, Stalin, is not the first and the best....'

(The words of Nikolai Bukharin, 1936)

8 | War

By the end of the 1930s Stalin's position inside his own country was stronger than it had ever been, but the spread of his **purges** to the **Red Army** from 1937 to 1939 – which involved the shooting of thousands of officers – seriously weakened the country's ability to defend itself. This was particularly dangerous at a time when the threats from outside – particularly from the strong and violently anti-**Communist** Nazi Germany – seemed to be growing almost by the day.

Playing for time

Stalin did his best to counter these threats. After 1934 he encouraged **Communists** in foreign countries to join with others on the left in **anti-Fascist popular fronts**; in 1936 he sent 'volunteers' to fight against the **Fascist** in the **Spanish Civil War**. He tried to create an anti-German alliance with the British and French. But all these efforts failed, and the Germans grew ever stronger and more dangerous.

When the British and French did not even invite the Soviet Union to the **Munich Conference** in 1938, Stalin became convinced that they were trying to push the Germans eastwards, against his own country. He responded a year later by signing the **Nazi–Soviet Pact** with Germany, which he expected would have the opposite effect of entangling Germany in a war with Britain and France. This, he calculated, would give him more time to repair the damage done to the Red Army by the purges. The division of Poland between Germany and the Soviet Union, which had been included in the Pact, also meant moving the Russian border 320 kilometres (200 miles) to the west. If the Germans did attack Russia in the future, their troops would have further to go to reach Moscow.

▲ *German Foreign Minister von Ribbentrop, Stalin and Soviet Foreign Minister Molotov at the signing of the Nazi–Soviet pact in August 1939.*

Shock and recovery

There is no reason to think that Stalin expected the Pact to last for ever, but he probably hoped that the British and French would keep the Germans occupied for longer than two years. He was certainly far from ready when the Germans did attack the Soviet Union in June 1941, and seems to have spent several days trying to persuade himself that it was not really happening. He had ignored warnings from the British in the days leading up to the attack, and he failed to give any clear instructions to his commanders in the front line. When the Germans easily broke through the Soviet lines and took hundreds of thousands of prisoners, he fell into a rage, blaming everyone but himself. He had many generals shot.

FINLAND

Leningrad
(St Petersburg)

Baltic Sea

ESTONIA

N
W — E
S

LATVIA

LITHUANIA

Moscow

GERMANY

Smolensk

SOVIET UNION

Key
- - - Front line Nov. 1942
- - - Front line Dec. 1943

POLAND

Kursk

Yoronezh

0   600 km
0   400 miles

Kiev

Stalingrad
(Volgograd)

Caspian Sea

Odessa

ROMANIA

Black
Sea

Grozny   Oilfields

▲ Germany's attack on the Soviet Union.

It was almost two weeks before he spoke to the Soviet people, but when he did he succeeded in striking the right note. 'Comrades, citizens, brothers and sisters,' he began, as if the Russian people were one big family. He did not tell his listeners they were fighting for Communism or **collectivization of agriculture** or his own 'universal genius' – he told them they were fighting a 'Great Patriotic War' for eternal Mother Russia, just like the one their ancestors had fought against Napoleon and the French 130 years earlier. Napoleon had failed and so would Hitler. The Russian people would never surrender.

During these first terrible months of the war, when the German armies looked unstoppable, one of the many Soviet officers captured was Stalin's son Yakov. The Germans offered to exchange him for some of their captured officers but Stalin refused. In his eyes Yakov had failed, had become a traitor by letting himself be captured, and Stalin disowned him. Yakov killed himself in captivity not long afterwards.

Running the war

As summer gave way to autumn, an early German victory looked more and more likely. Three things prevented it. One was the earliest winter in living memory, which first clogged the roads with mud and then with snow, slowing the tanks to a crawl. A second was the Germans' own behaviour. In many areas they were welcomed, but they treated everyone so viciously that soon even Stalin's **dictatorship** looked a better bet.

Stalin was lucky on both these counts, but he could claim some credit for the third block to the Germans' progress – the Red Army's ability to fight on, despite losing so much territory and so many industrial plants. It was able to do so because most of the armament factories had been moved east of Moscow, where they were still a long way beyond the Germans' reach.

In late November the Germans were thrown back from the outer suburbs of Moscow. It is hard to say whether Stalin's decision to stay in the **Kremlin** through these critical days inspired the Red Army units defending the capital, but it does seem fairly certain that his departure would have dealt a terrible blow to their confidence.

Stalin was far from a physical coward, and he also proved himself quite competent when it came to military strategy. Early in the campaign a state defence committee – Stavka – was set up to run the Soviet war machine, with Stalin, needless to say, at its head. This committee took all the key military decisions over the next three and a half years, and since most of these proved reasonably good decisions, Stalin deserves some credit as a war leader. If he did not always know what to do himself, he was good at picking and listening to generals who did.

Stalingrad and after

When the Germans launched a huge attack in the spring of 1942, the Soviets did not repeat their mistake of 1941. Instead of trying to hold its ground and ending up encircled by German tanks, the Red Army simply retreated, drawing the enemy further and further into the vast open spaces of the Soviet Union. Hitler was determined that his armies should take the city of Stalingrad, thinking that this would be a symbolic defeat for Stalin himself.

The Red Army lured the Germans on, until there were almost half a million men fighting each other in the ruins of the city. And then the trap was sprung. In November more Soviet armies, supplied with tanks and guns from the factories which had been moved to the east, encircled and cut off the German troops. Two horrifying months later they surrendered. It was a blow from which the German army never really recovered.

From that moment on, the Red Army's eventual triumph was never really in doubt. There were a few temporary setbacks, but the Germans were steadily forced back towards their own

▲ *Soldiers of the Red Army fighting amidst the ruins of Stalingrad, October 1942. Three months later the surrender of the German army trapped in the city signalled a turning point of the war.*

borders and beyond. In April 1945 the Red Army finally captured the German capital, Berlin. By this time Stalin had long since left the day-to-day direction of the armies to his generals. He was concentrating on making sure that the Soviets did well out of the coming peace.

Key dates: World War II in Russia

1941	• June–Nov.	The Germans advance 960 kilometres (600 miles) into Soviet territory, but are stopped outside Moscow and Leningrad. The siege of Leningrad will last 900 days.
1942	• June–Nov.	German advance in the south fails to reach the Caucasus oilfields or capture Stalingrad
	• Nov.–Jan. 1943	A large German army is cut off and captured in Stalingrad. From this point on the Red Army holds the initiative.
1943	• July–Aug.	The battle of Kursk, the greatest tank battle in history, is won by the Red Army
1943	• Dec.– April 1945	The Red Army throws the Germans out of the Soviet Union and drives all the way to Berlin

During the war, vast areas of **European Russia** and the Ukraine had been laid waste, with farms, industries and communications completely destroyed. After the dramatic progress of the 1930s it seemed as if the country was almost back to square one. The Soviet Union needed a huge rebuilding programme, and that could only be carried through if the country was not being threatened from outside. So Stalin's first objective at the peace negotiations was to make his country safe. The most important things he wanted were a weak, divided Germany and friendly governments in those European countries, like Poland and Romania, which bordered his own.

Wishful thinking and misunderstandings

In Britain and the USA there was much good will towards Stalin and the Soviet people. Most people in the West realized how much the Soviet Union had suffered at the Germans' hands, and Stalin himself – or 'Uncle Joe' as he was often affectionately known – was considered an heroic figure. Few people in the West knew the extent of Stalin's crimes inside the Soviet Union, and there was a great reluctance to think of him as a new enemy, or to worry about the possibility of another war, this time between themselves and the Soviet Union.

Three conferences were held by the Big Three powers (Britain, USA and the Soviet Union) to decide the shape of the post-war world – at Tehran in Iran in 1943, and Yalta in the Crimea (now Ukraine) and Potsdam in Germany in 1945. At each of these meetings Stalin and the Western leaders reached informal agreements which seemed to satisfy them. But in the end these agreements proved worthless for one simple reason – they were based on the idea that all the powers could get what they needed and wanted. They couldn't. It was like telling two people that one could have a blue room and one could have a red room when there was only one room to begin with. You could have a Poland which was friendly to the Soviet Union or you could have a Poland which was part of a **free enterprise** Europe. You could not have both.

For several months after the war the two sides tried to convince themselves and each other that everything would work out, but after a while they both began to feel betrayed. At the Yalta conference Stalin had promised that he would not support **Communists** in countries like Greece, which lay outside those areas he considered crucial for the security of the Soviet Union, and he kept those promises. All over the world the war had given a boost to local Communist parties, and the situation was much more promising for world revolution than it had been in the early 1920s. But Stalin remained faithful to '**Socialism** in one country', and did virtually nothing to help them.

▼ *Stalin representing the Soviet Union and Winston Churchill representing Britain in Yalta in 1945.*

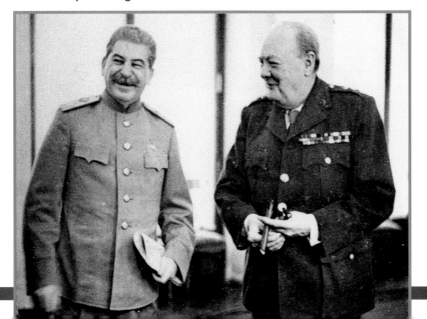

Dividing up the world

'I wrote out on a half-sheet of paper:
Romania: Russia 90%, others 10%
Greece: Great Britain (in accord with USA) 90%, Russia 10%
Yugoslavia: 50–50%
Hungary: 50–50%
Bulgaria: Russia 75%, the others 25%.
I pushed this across to Stalin... there was a slight pause. Then
he took his blue pencil and made a large tick upon it and
passed it back to us. It was all settled in no more time than it
takes to set it down.'

(Winston Churchill, remembering the way he and Stalin
divided up eastern Europe at a Moscow meeting in October 1944)

Accepting the inevitable

It slowly became clear to Stalin that the Americans were not playing ball. They had agreed to share the secret of how to make the atomic bomb but now refused to do so, even though many important people in both Britain and the USA thought that they should. In the summer of 1945 they suddenly stopped sending **Lend-Lease** aid to the Soviet Union. When, two years later, they offered more economic help as part of their **Marshall Plan** package for the whole of Europe, they asked Stalin to accept conditions which he found both insulting and threatening. These included opening Russia to Western inspectors and a guarantee of American property rights in eastern Europe. And when the Americans tried to bribe the Poles and Romanians into accepting similar conditions it looked as if they were deliberately trying to turn the Soviet Union's neighbours into the Soviet Union's enemies.

▲ *An American transport plane comes in to land at Berlin's Tempelhof Airport in August 1948. Stalin attempted to control all of Berlin by closing all roads and railways, but he could not stop Western planes from airlifting in supplies.*

Stalin fought back. The **Red Army** was still occupying most of eastern Europe, and he used its presence to install Communist governments in one country after another. With party **dictatorships**, **planned economies** and **collectivization of agriculture**, these countries were sealed off from the free enterprise world as completely as the Soviet Union was. It was the only certain way to keep them friendly.

The Americans saw this as Communist aggression, and the two sides gave up any pretence that their practical differences could be sorted out around a conference table. Instead they both began to emphasize their **ideological differences** and to compete with each other all over the world, wherever their supporters came into conflict. Stalin was probably happier with this **Cold War** than he had been with such an uncertain peace. It was his world against theirs. He could control his world, and keep theirs at a distance.

The eight years which passed between the end of World War II and Stalin's death in March 1953 were years of intense economic activity in the Soviet Union. The factories and dams and railways destroyed by the Germans were re-built, and new ones grew up beside them. For the second time in 20 years the Soviet people set out to lay the foundations of a prosperous future. In the Soviet media the achievements of people and party in both war and peace were continually praised and celebrated.

These really were extraordinary achievements, but Stalin took no risks. He made sure his people had nothing to compare them with. **Red Army** soldiers returning from duty in eastern Europe were forbidden to talk about what they had seen; the newspapers either ignored or lied about life in the West; and hardly any Soviet citizens were allowed to travel abroad.

МЫ ИДЕМ ДАЛЬШЕ, ВПЕРЕД, К КОММУНИЗМУ.
И. В. СТАЛИН.

The mixture as before

Stalin himself was more of a **dictator** than ever. He hardly ever appeared in public, and made few speeches. He lived mostly at one of his **dachas** outside Moscow, and took a long holiday on the Black Sea coast each autumn.

◀ *Lenin looks approvingly over Stalin's shoulder in a 1950 Soviet propaganda poster.*

There was no longer any pretence of collective (group) leadership – the ruling **Politburo** and the party's **Central Committee** did not even meet between 1947 and 1952. Stalin decided what he wanted to happen, and the necessary instructions were passed on to the Soviet people by his small band of faithful colleagues.

Stalin's touch

'When I felt his handshake it was like being struck by lightning. I hid my hand inside my coat cuff, got into my car and rushed home. Without stopping to answer my worried wife's questions I went to the cot where my small son was sleeping, stretched out my hand and rubbed his head with it, so that he too would feel the warmth of Stalin's touch.'

(Yuri Borisov, an important industrial manager in the 1940s, on meeting Stalin)

At the same time his **personality cult** reached new heights of absurdity. The newspaper *Pravda* had this advice for its readers in February 1950: 'If you meet with difficulties in your work, or suddenly doubt your abilities, think of him – of Stalin – and you will find the confidence you need. If you feel tired in an hour when you should not, think of him – of Stalin – and your work will go well.'

But no amount of power, no extremes of praise, could make him feel safe. 'Everywhere and in everything he saw "enemies", "two-facers" and spies,' one of his supporters said years later. In 1948 Stalin ordered a new **purge**, and 1000 party members were shot in Leningrad. For most of the next five years those nearest to him lived in fear. They knew only too well what had happened to Stalin's colleagues in the past.

No second chances

'The terrible thing about Stalin was that if you made a mistake with him, it was like mishandling a detonator – it was the last mistake of your life. Stalin was terrible because he never listened to excuses. He never even accused you; the only sign was a malignant gleam from his yellow, tigerish eyes and a slight puckering of his lower eyelids. Inwardly he had already passed sentence without the victim being aware of it: he would be allowed to leave, he would be arrested the same night, and by morning he would be shot.'

(Russian writer Alexander Solzhenitsyn, who spent many years in Stalin's prison camps. Several of his books paint a vivid and harrowing picture of life inside these camps)

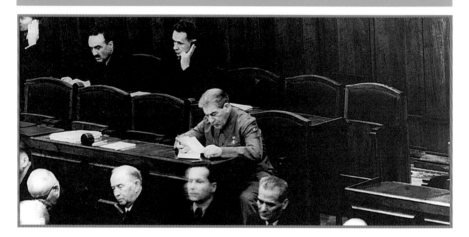

▲ *Stalin attends the Nineteenth Congress of the Russian Communist Party, October 1952.*

A bad end

Early in 1953 a group of **Kremlin** doctors were suddenly arrested and charged with poisoning a minor party leader some years before, and it seemed almost certain that a new and terrible **purge** was about to begin. But before this could happen Stalin suffered the first of two strokes. Three days later, on 5 March, he died.

'The death agony was terrible,' his daughter said later. 'He literally choked to death as we watched. At what seemed like the very last moment he suddenly opened his eyes and cast a glance over everyone in the room. It was a terrible glance, insane or perhaps angry and full of fear of death.'

His colleagues hardly bothered to conceal their relief. In the country's **labour camps** the news of his death raised hopes that the long nightmare was over. For all the people of the Soviet Union it felt as if an era had ended, but after more than 20 years of Stalin-worship it was also hard to imagine the world without him. Hundreds of thousands came from all over the Soviet Union to attend his funeral, and many were killed in the mad crush of weeping mourners.

▲ *A bank of flowers lines the Kremlin wall on either side of the mausoleum where Stalin's body has been placed beside Lenin's, March 1953.*

No one knows exactly how many Soviet citizens died premature deaths while Stalin ruled over them. The best bet is that between 15 and 20 million people perished during the period of **collectivization**, forced industrialization and the great **purge** (1929–38). Some died of starvation, some from ill-treatment and some were executed, but they all died as a direct and predictable result of Stalin's policies. He was the one of the greatest mass murderers in human history.

Comparisons are often made between Stalin and the German leader Hitler, who was also criminally responsible for millions of deaths. The one obvious difference lay in their aims. Hitler looked no further than a world of masters and slaves; Stalin, at least in the beginning, believed in creating a fairer world for everyone. This does not excuse Stalin's terrible crimes, but it does make it important to understand them. In the beginning the various ideologies of Marxism, **Socialism** and **Communism** were all concerned with the ending of poverty and injustice, with introducing greater equality between people, and with promoting a version of freedom that was rooted in fairness. The fact that **Marxist Socialists** took over the government of Russia meant that Socialism came to be associated with what happened in that country. So one consequence of Stalin's crimes was to discredit, or at least to raise grave doubts about, Socialism as a way forward for humanity.

Stalin's contribution
It is important to separate out Stalin's personal contribution, to work out which things he alone was responsible for. Both Lenin and Trotsky were willing to use terror against their enemies, and Trotsky argued for a forced industrialization

programme before Stalin did. Any of the three might have introduced the system of economic planning, and allowed the death of democracy which accompanied it.

What set Stalin apart was his lack of restraint. He was not held back – as Lenin and Trotsky both were – by any sympathy for other human beings, and he was always terrified of losing the power he had. It was his warped personality that cost so many millions their lives.

There was at least something to show for all the sacrifice. Fifty years of industrialization were crammed into ten, and this growth was essential to the country's success in World War II, a success that the rest of the world had good reason to be grateful for. There were also important elements of Socialism's original promise in the free universal health care and education systems that were set up, and in the guarantee of jobs for everyone.

FOR DETAILS ON KEY PEOPLE OF STALIN'S TIME, SEE PAGES 58–9.

After his death

When Stalin died his successors thought they could abandon the bad parts of his system – the **dictatorship** and the terror – and build on the achievements. At the Twentieth Party Congress in 1956 the Soviet leader Nikita Khrushchev criticized Stalin's 'excesses' and announced that the party would be 'de-Stalinized'. But the system of central planning was not changed, and over the next 20 years it became obvious that it was not working as they had hoped. Stalin's system was good at getting modernization started, at doing simple things such as increasing steel production and building railways, but when it came to the complex economy of the late 20th century, with its millions of different types of goods, it could not cope. There were just too many possibilities for the planners to include in their plans.

While there was still hope that the system would come up with the goods, most of the Soviet people were willing to put up with its less attractive aspects, like the lack of freedom. But when it finally became obvious in the 1980s that the system was an economic failure, there was no good reason to keep it. The last Soviet leader, Mikhail Gorbachev, tried to make it more democratic, but he was too late. By 1991 Stalin's system of central planning was being dismantled in all those countries in which it had been installed. It had failed to provide either a fairer or a more efficient way of organizing society

▲ A statue of Stalin lies broken on the ground after the fall of Communism in the Soviet Union in 1991.

Today

And yet, despite the failure, Stalin remains a popular figure for many people, particularly in Russia. Why is this? Why should a man who imposed so many sacrifices on others, and yet still failed to produce a successful system, still have his picture carried through the streets of Moscow?

The transition to democracy has been difficult, and life in present-day Russia is chaotic and uncertain. Ordinary people thought they knew where they were with Stalin. They knew they had a job, that the streets were safe, that as long as they kept their heads down there would be no knock on the door. There was order. They were being looked after. And during Stalin's day the Soviet Union was becoming daily richer, daily more powerful. In the prison camps beyond the Arctic Circle millions were being worked to death, but for most Russians the future may have seemed more promising then than it does today.

▶ A Communist rally in Moscow in July 1999. More than 46 years after Stalin's death, these demonstrators still waved a red flag with his image on it.

Timeline

1878	Soso Djugashvili (later called Stalin) is born in Gori. It was thought until recently that he was born the following year.
1893	Attends the theological seminary (school for training priests) in Tiflis.
1898	Russian Social Democratic Workers Party formed.
1899	Djugashvili is expelled from the seminary and gets a job at the Tiflis observatory.
1901	After helping to organize a political demonstration in Tiflis, finds himself on the run from the police.
1902	After organizing a demonstration in Batum, is arrested and exiled to Siberia.
1903	Russian Social Democratic Workers Party splits into **Bolshevik** and **Menshevik** parties.
1904	Djugashvili returns to Tiflis and marries Ektarina.
1905	Meets Lenin for the first time in Finland.
1906	First son (Yakov) is born.
1907	Djugashvili organizes and probably takes part in the Erevan Square gold robbery. His first wife dies.
1908–12	He is arrested, exiled and manages to escape four times.
1913	Meets Lenin in Cracow and travels to Vienna with him. With Lenin's help, writes 'Marxism and the National Question', signing it 'Stalin' – his new name. Back in Russia he is arrested again.
1914	World War I begins.
1917	First Russian revolution takes place in February. Stalin travels to Moscow. Second Russian revolution – the Bolshevik revolution – takes place in October.
1918	Marries Nadezhda Alliluyeva.
1918–21	Russian civil war. Stalin is sent first to Tsaritsyn, and then to Petrograd and the Ukraine.

For details on key people of Stalin's time, see pages 58–9.

1921	Second son (Vasili) is born.
1922	Stalin becomes General Secretary of the **Communist** Party.
1924	Lenin dies in January leaving a Testament critical of Stalin. Other party leaders choose to ignore it.
1925–27	In alliance with Bukharin, Stalin defeats the 'Left Opposition' led by Trotsky and Zinoviev.
1926	Daughter (Svetlana) is born.
1927–29	Stalin defeats so-called 'Right Opposition' led by Bukharin.
1928–29	First **five-year plan** formulated.
1929–33	**Collectivization of agriculture**. 'Liquidation of the **kulaks**'.
1932	Second wife (Nadezhda) commits suicide.
1934	Stalin uses Sergei Kirov's assassination in Leningrad as excuse to begin a purge of the party.
1936	Sends 'volunteers' to fight in **Spanish Civil War**.
1937–39	Period of **Red Army purges**.
1938	Munich Conference.
1939	Signs **Nazi–Soviet Pact** with Hitler.
1941	Germany attacks the Soviet Union. German armies are stopped at gates of Leningrad and Moscow.
1942	Second great German offensive is stopped at Stalingrad.
1943–45	Red Army slowly forces German army back to Berlin. Stalin meets other two allied leaders at Tehran (1943), Yalta (1945) and Potsdam (1945).
1945	World War II ends. USA ends **Lend-Lease** programme.
1947	**Cold War** begins in earnest.
1948	Stalin purges the party in Leningrad.
1953	Dies at the age of 75.

Key people of Stalin's time

Beria, Lavrenti (1899–1953). Georgian supporter of Stalin and head of Soviet secret police from 1938. After Stalin's death Beria was accused of attempting to seize power and executed.

Bukharin, Nikolai Ivanovich (1888–1938). Born in Moscow, Bukharin became politically active as a student during the 1905 revolution. He lived as a **revolutionary** inside Russia until 1911, when he was arrested and **exiled**. He escaped to western Europe and returned to Russia in 1917. While there was a chance of further revolutions in Europe he argued for the **Bolsheviks** to make trouble wherever they could, but when it became clear that these revolutions would not take place, he joined first Lenin and then Stalin in arguing for a slow and peaceful progress towards **Socialism** in Russia. He was eventually driven from power when Stalin decided to adopt the faster method of modernizing the country. In 1938 he was the main figure in the last of the great **show trials**, and was shot soon afterwards.

Churchill, Sir Winston (1874–1965). British politician. During the 1930s Churchill spoke out against the policy of successive British governments. He became prime minister during the crucial early phase of World War II, and proved an inspirational figure in British defiance of Nazi Germany.

Hitler, Adolf (1889–1945). Leader of the German National Socialist Party (1921–45) and Führer (**dictator**) of Germany from 1933 until he committed suicide in April 1945. Hitler restored the German economy and German pride through rearmament and an aggressive determination to retrieve territory lost in World War I. He was primarily responsible for the outbreak of World War II and the subsequent killing of 6 million Jews in German-occupied Europe.

Lenin (1870–1924). Born Vladimir Ilyich Ulyanov. While practising law at **St Petersburg**, Lenin's interest in revolutionary politics developed. He was exiled to Siberia (1897–1900), and spent the following seventeen years living in western Europe. He was a deep thinker and wrote a great deal about politics and economics. He provoked the split in the Russian Social Democratic Workers Party in 1903 and became the undisputed leader of the Bolshevik Party.

He returned to Russia in March 1917 and led the revolution in October that brought the Bolsheviks to power. Soon after the civil war had been won in 1921 he became ill, and he spent much of his last two years worrying about where the revolution was headed. He died in January 1924, leaving behind a 'Testament' which suggested the removal of Stalin from his post of party general secretary.

Marx, Karl (1818–83). German philosopher, economist and political scientist whose theories of social development helped to inspire both Socialism and Communism.

Molotov, Vyacheslav (1890–1986). Early member of Bolsheviks, who became a firm supporter of Stalin after Lenin's death. He was Soviet foreign minister in 1939–49 and 1953–56.

Trotsky, Leon (1879–1940). Born Lev Davidovich Bronstein in Yanovka, Ukraine. As a young Jewish revolutionary, he was arrested and exiled to Siberia in 1898. He escaped to western Europe in 1902, but returned to play a starring role as leader of the St Petersburg Soviet (Council) of Workers' Deputies in the 1905 Russian revolution. A great speaker and writer, he worked as a journalist in the West until 1917, when he returned again to Russia. He joined the Bolsheviks, supported Lenin when he argued for a Bolshevik revolution, and played a major role in bringing that revolution about. As Lenin's Commissar of War he created the **Red Army** and led it to victory in the civil war. After Lenin's death he argued for spreading the revolution to other countries, and was eased from power by jealous colleagues and the single-minded Stalin. Though expelled from the Soviet Union in 1929, he continued to oppose Stalin in his writings. In 1940 he was killed by one of Stalin's agents in Mexico.

Zinoviev, Grigory (1883–1936). One of the most important Bolshevik leaders before the revolution. He was head of the Communist International, the association of national Communist Parties, from 1919 to 1926. He supported Stalin against Trotsky after Lenin's death, but was then defeated by an alliance of Stalin and Bukharin. He was executed by Stalin after the first of the great show trials in 1936.

Places to visit and further reading

Place to visit
Imperial War Museum Duxford, Cambridgeshire CB2 4QU

Websites
BBC history website:
   www.bbc.co.uk/education/modern/stalin/stalihtm.htm
Biographical article on the internet:
   russianculture.about.com/culture/russianculture/library/weekly/
   aa031698.htm
Detailed biographical article from the Grolier Online Encyclopedia:
   gi.grolier.com/wwii/wwii_stalin. htlm
Educational website from the ThinkQuest Library of Entries:
   library.thinkquest.org/17120/data/bios/stalin
Educational website provided by the UK Public Records Office:
   learningcurve.pro.gov.uk/heroesvillains/stalin
Heinemann Explore, an online resource for Key Stage 3 History:
   www.heinemannexploresec.com

Further reading
Animal Farm, George Orwell, Penguin, 2000
The Cold War (20th Century Perspectives series), David Taylor,
   Heinemann Library, 2001
Key Battles of World War II (20th Century Perspectives series), Fiona
   Reynoldson, Heinemann Library, 2001
Russia 1905–56, Nigel Kelly, Heinemann, 1998
The Twentieth Century World (Living Through History series), Nigel
   Kelly, Rosemary Rees and Jane Shuter, Heinemann Library, 1998

Sources
Joseph Stalin, John Laver, Hodder, 1994
Memories of a Revolutionary, Victor Serge, Oxford University Press,
   1963
Stalin, Edward Radzinsky, Sceptre, 1997
Stalin, Isaac Deutscher, Pelican, 1966
Stalin and the Soviet Union, Josh Brooman, Longman, 1989
The Russian Revolution, Tamara Pimlott, Thomas Nelson, 1986
The Second World War, Vol. 6, Winston Churchill, Cassell, 1951
Three Who Made a Revolution, Bertram Wolfe, Pelican, 1966

Glossary

anti-Fascist popular front alliance of Social democrats and Communists against Fascists

autonomous having some degree of self-government inside a wider political body

black market unofficial, and often illegal, buying and selling

Bolsheviks one of the two political parties that emerged from the 1903 split in the Russian Social Democratic Workers Party. *Bolsheviks* is Russian for 'those with a majority'.

bourgeoisie the capitalist class – those who own the industries and banks

Central Committee after 1917, the committee elected by local Communist Party committees throughout the Soviet Union

civil war war between different groups in one country

Cold War name given to the hostility that existed between the free enterprise and Communist worlds between 1947 and the late 1980s.

collectivization of agriculture the creation of large, jointly-owned farms by joining together small farms, which had previously been privately owned

Commissar for Nationalities position of authority with particular responsibility for relations between the different ethnic groups that made up the population of the Soviet Union

Communism according to Karl Marx, the stage of history that would follow Socialism. In this stage, free people would share with each other in a situation of economic plenty. The name was adopted by the Bolsheviks and came to be associated with the system of economic planning and political dictatorship developed in the Soviet Union in the mid-20th century.

Cossacks a people of southern Russia

czar (or tsar) hereditary ruler of the Russian Empire

dacha Russian country cottage used as a weekend or holiday home

delegate elected representative

dictatorship government by an individual (called a dictator) or small group that does not allow the mass of the people any say

European Russia that part of Russia lying to the west of the Ural Mountains (see map on page 13)

exile being sent away as punishment. In czarist Russia, exile to remote and inhospitable parts of the country like Siberia was a common punishment.

Fascism dictatorial system of government which came to be known for its aggressive nationalism

five-year plan plan of all intended economic activity over a five-year period. The first Soviet five-year plan was formulated in 1928.

free enterprise organization of economy where individuals rather than governments make the decisions about which goods and services are produced, and how they are bought and sold

ideological differences disagreements over how economies and societies should be organized

industrial goods goods made from raw materials or other goods in factories or workshops

Kremlin walled fortress in Moscow that has been the traditional home of Russian leaders through the centuries

kulak rich peasant – in many cases, an employer of other peasants

labour camp camp where prisoners were forced to work

Lend-Lease programme of American aid to those countries fighting the Germans, which began even before the USA entered the war in 1941

market rate price which a buyer and seller would agree on if there was no intervention from government

Marshall Plan huge programme of American aid to the countries of Europe, proposed in 1947 and put into operation in 1948–52

Marxist Socialist Socialist who believes and acts according to the theories of Karl Marx. (See information boxes on pages 11 and 16.)

Mensheviks one of the two political parties that emerged from the 1903 split in the Russian Social Democratic Workers Party. *Mensheviks* is Russian for 'those in a minority'.

modernization bringing up to date by making use of the most advanced technology available

Munich Conference conference held in September 1938 to decide the future of Czechoslovakia, after Germany had threatened to invade that country. Britain and France offered a compromise, which gave the Germans only a part of the country.

Nazi–Soviet Pact treaty signed by Nazi Germany and the Soviet Union in August 1939. They agreed not to attack each other and to remain neutral if the other was involved in war with another country.

peasant small farmer or farm worker

personality cult campaign of exaggerated praise for an individual

Politburo Soviet cabinet (or small ruling committee elected by the Central Committee)

planned economy economy in which all decisions are taken by a central authority, and not by the free workings of the market

political police police concerned with countering threats to the government

purge in a political party, a clearing out of unacceptable members. In Stalin's time this often involved having them killed.

Red Army originally the army formed by the Bolsheviks to defend their revolution in the civil war. After the civil war it became the official army of the Soviet Union.

Red Guards armed supporters of the Bolshevik revolution in its early years

reign of terror sustained campaign of violence and intimidation

revolutionary in politics, working to overthrow the existing order in its entirety – not just swapping one group of individuals for another

St Petersburg city on the Gulf of Finland, capital of the Russian Empire. Renamed Petrograd in 1914, Leningrad in 1924, and St Petersburg once more in 1991.

show trial trial held in public, to make a point to those outside the courtroom

smallpox serious and often fatal disease, common in the late 19th century.

Socialism way of organizing society that puts the needs of the community above the short-term wants or needs of the individual

Spanish Civil War civil war (1936–39) in Spain between republican government forces (mostly Socialists and Communists) and rebel Fascist forces

underground war when opponents of a government try to operate a hidden campaign, keeping their identity and whereabouts secret

White Army army fighting against the Bolsheviks in the civil war. Some White Armies wanted to bring back the czar; others to restore the government which existed between the two revolutions in 1917.

Index